Getting To Know
Your Hamster

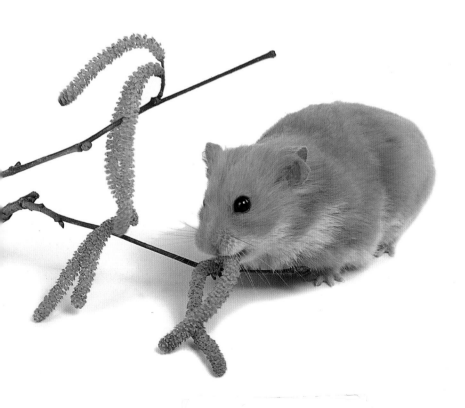

Getting To Know Your Hamster

Gill Page

INTERPET PUBLISHING

The Author

Gill Page has been involved with a wide variety of animals for many years. She has run a successful pet centre and for some time helped in rescuing and re-homing unwanted animals. She has cared for many animals of her own and is keen to pass on her experience so that children may learn how to look after their pets lovingly and responsibly.

Published by Interpet Publishing,
Vincent Lane,
Dorking,
Surrey RH4 3YX,
England

© 2000 Interpet Publishing Ltd.
This reprint 2007

ISBN 978-1-84286-112-7

The recommendations in this book are given without any guarantees on the part of the author and publisher. If in doubt, seek the advice of a vet or pet-care specialist.

Credits

Editor: Philip de Ste. Croix

Designer: Phil Clucas MSIAD

Studio photography: Neil Sutherland

Colour artwork: Rod Ferring

Production management: Consortium, Poslingford, Suffolk CO10 8RA

Print production: SNP Leefung China

Printed and bound in the Far East

Contents

Making Friends

Hello. I am your new friend. What is your name? You can give me a short name and then I will know when you are calling me. If I tell you lots of things about myself, you will know how to take good care of me. I want a home of my own that is safe and cosy. I will take a little time to get used to you and then we will be very good friends.

I am a fast runner and like to escape from my cage if you don't shut it properly.

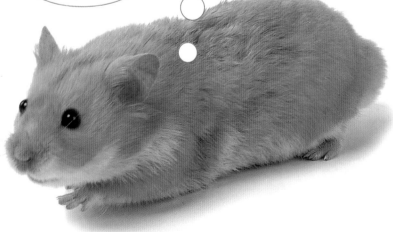

I have thick, soft hair and shiny black eyes. I keep myself very clean; you can help too by brushing me. I am very fussy – I like my house kept clean and tidy. I want to live on my own. I do not like sharing my house with anybody else. I like fresh food and water every day. I sleep in the daytime and play at night. I may be very small, but I am very brave. My favourite game is escaping from my cage! I might be tiny but I need lots of exercise. If I lived in the wild, I would run and run for miles every night. I can have long or short hair which can grow in lots of different colours.

Getting To Know Me

I am tiny, but very quick. When I first come to live with you, I will weigh about 90 grams (3oz). My fur is usually short and shiny. Some of my friends have really long hair, but they are much harder to look after. They have to be brushed every day. I can be all one colour, mostly a golden brown with a white tummy, or a mixture of colours. I am called a Syrian, or Golden, hamster. You can buy two other sorts of hamster. One is called a Chinese hamster. He looks a bit like a mouse. The other is the Russian hamster. He is small, fluffy and round. I'll tell you more about them at the end of this book.

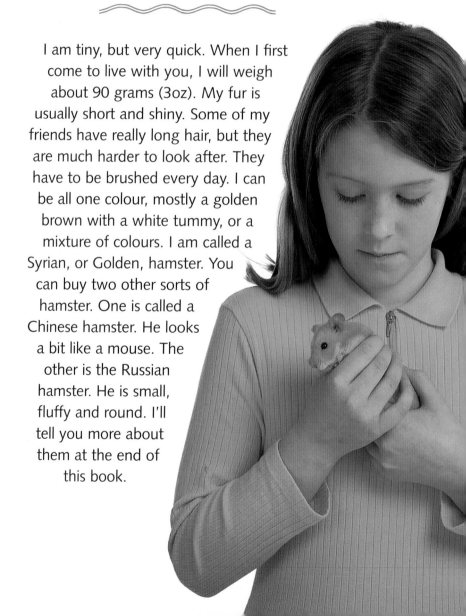

I am a Russian hamster, and smaller than my Syrian relative.

I have four toes on each of my front feet and five on the back ones. My teeth keep growing all the time. I must have lots of things to chew to keep them short. Please pick me up carefully. If you grab me and lift me up quickly, it feels as if a big monster has swooped down and carried me away. That really scares me. Slide one hand under me and cup the other round the front of my body. Hold me gently close to you. Please don't drop me.

I have five toes on my back feet.

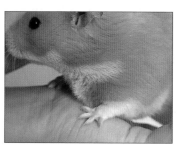

But only four toes on my front feet.

Taking Me Home

Buy me from a pet shop or a breeder. Sometimes animal rescue centres have a few of us that need good homes. I must be five weeks old before you may take me home. If you have never had a friend like me before, it is best to choose one of us with short hair. We are much easier to look after than long-haired hamsters. I should have a shiny coat, no bald patches nor any insects in my fur. My eyes must be bright and shiny and my nose should be clean.

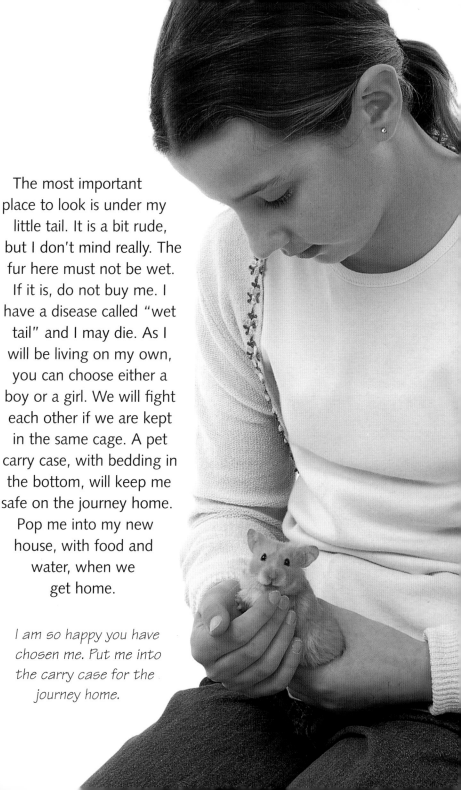

The most important place to look is under my little tail. It is a bit rude, but I don't mind really. The fur here must not be wet. If it is, do not buy me. I have a disease called "wet tail" and I may die. As I will be living on my own, you can choose either a boy or a girl. We will fight each other if we are kept in the same cage. A pet carry case, with bedding in the bottom, will keep me safe on the journey home. Pop me into my new house, with food and water, when we get home.

I am so happy you have chosen me. Put me into the carry case for the journey home.

Settling Me In

I will be frightened for a while when I first get home and will probably hide in my bedding. I sleep all day, waking up in the evening. When I think that nobody is looking, I will sneak out to explore. I will look round my cage and have some food and a drink. Leave me alone, just feed and water me and keep the cage clean. Don't try and pick me up for a while. I know I am small, but I am very brave. I'm sorry – but I will bite you if I think you are going to hurt me. I have to learn to trust you. When I do, I will happily let you pick me up.

Once I have grown to trust you, we will become friends.

Daytime is my bedtime. I get cross if I am woken up when I am fast asleep. Do you? After about two weeks you can start to make friends with me. Stroke me with one finger. Later put a treat in your hand and stretch your hand into my cage. I might sit on your hand and try and taste you with my teeth. Keep very still and I will not bite. If I stand on my back legs and make a noise, I am still scared. Keep trying – I'm sure we'll soon be friends.

My Own House

I will spend a lot of my time in my house – so please buy me a nice big one. I am very naughty and I am always trying to escape, so make sure the cage is made for hamsters. I am awake all night so I need lots of room to run around and play while you are asleep. Most of the cages you can buy are made of wire with a plastic base. Some fun ones are also made of wire and plastic, but you can add tunnels and playrooms to them.

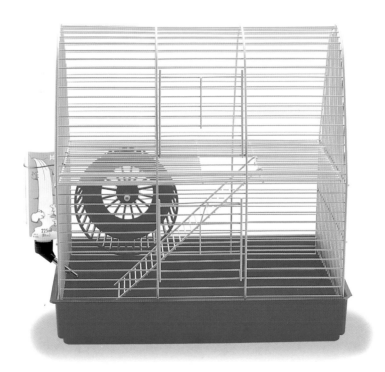

A box within my cage makes an ideal nest site for me.

A large fish tank can be made into a nice home for me.
It will need a wire top clipped onto it. The tank must not
be too deep though. If it is, it will get too hot and stuffy
inside and will make me ill. I need a room to sleep in.
I just love making nests and digging tunnels. It is when
I get bored that I try to escape. You hate sitting still in the
same place for a long time, don't you? My home must
be kept inside your house, and set high off the floor.
I cannot live outside. I must not get cold – I will die.

Time For Bed

There are all sorts of things you can use for my bedding. I don't sleep with sheets and duvets like you do. I like soft, sweet-smelling hay. I can eat it and sleep on it too. I can burrow into it when I am scared. Bedding that is made just for me is fun. You can buy paper bedding or fluffy, soft stuff. I make a cosy, little nest with this.

I like my nest to be snuggly and warm

Shredded paper

Nestle down

Wood shavings

Wool fibre

Use wood shavings in the bottom of my house. This will soak up any wet patches. The dirty bits will have to be changed every day. If you don't do this, it gets very smelly. I won't like that. You need only clean out the dirty bits and any old pieces of food that I have not eaten. If you have one, put them on the compost heap in the garden. Then add more clean bedding. Every week you can pop me into my carry case. This keeps me safe while you are sorting out my house. Clear all the bedding out. Wipe the cage out with a damp cloth or use cage wipes to make it smell sweet. Make sure the cage is dry before you put me and my bedding back in.

I like to nibble on nuts. They are good for my teeth too.

My Favourite Foods

Before you bring me home, ask about the food I have been eating. It is often a mixture and comes in a packet. Buy some of the same stuff to take home with me. Also ask if I have been allowed to eat fresh food. If I haven't, just give me a little bit to start with. I can have a little more each day, as long as it doesn't upset my tummy. A good diet for me is some hamster mix with extra fruit, nuts and vegetables.

Sprout tops

Vitamin drops

Hay

Hamster mix

Apple

Carrot

Parsnip

I like my food to be clean and fresh. When I eat, I push as much I can into my mouth. Inside, at each side of my mouth, I have a sort of pocket, called a pouch. I know it makes me look funny and fat-faced but it is my way of carrying my food back to my nest.

Some of the fresh foods I can eat are apples, pears, carrots and tomatoes. In the summer you can pick wild plants for me. Dandelion, groundsel and clover are good. Once or twice a week you can give me a tiny piece of hard cheese or even one or two mealworms which you can buy from a pet shop – yummy.

Nice Food, Nasty Food

I must tell you about a few of the things I must not eat. Some of them will make me feel really ill. There are things that are very bad for me, and they could even kill me. Never, ever, give me bracken, ragwort, buttercup or tomato leaves. There are other bad foods. Before you pick anything ask mummy or daddy to check it out. I do not like any food that has been picked from places that dogs and cats have used as a toilet. Yucky! There are lots of weeds and grass that I can eat, but I don't like the smell or taste of the stuff growing next to a road. I think the fumes from all those cars and lorries that drive by make it taste funny.

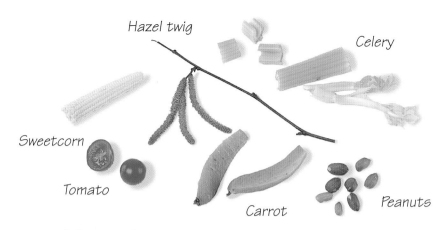

Hazel twig

Celery

Sweetcorn

Tomato

Carrot

Peanuts

Food that you have picked needs to be washed before you give it to me. There are a few vegetables that will give me a bit of a tummy ache. These are raw potatoes, leeks and white cabbage. I must not have too much lettuce or cucumber. Oranges and kiwi fruit can sometimes give me a pain in my tum. I like nibbling on nuts but one nut I must not eat is a "conker" from the horse chestnut tree. That's bad for me.

Celery and baby sweetcorn are yummy!

Meal Times

I like small, heavy dishes for my food. One for the dry food and one for my fruit and vegetables. I can be a bit silly and put my feet in the dish. If it is too big, I will walk all over my food. A dish that is made of pottery is easy to keep clean. I might chew up a plastic dish. I like to drink clean water every day. When I am eating hay, I get quite thirsty, but a water bottle lets me have a drink any time I need it. I may not drink very much, but I like to know it is there. The water keeps clean in a bottle, but if it is in a dish I often stand in it and make it dirty. Change the water daily and wash the bottle out every week.

I will need two heavy bowls and a drinking bottle for fresh water.

Feeding Timetable

I like to have my meals at the same time every day. I will know if you are late in feeding me! My dry food can be left in the cage all day. I can nibble at it when I feel hungry. Feed me in the morning and evening. I have a very small tummy. I only need about two, heaped teaspoonfuls of dry food. I always make a store of my food, so you will soon see if you are giving me too much.

Breakfast
A little bit of hamster mix.

Dinner
Top up my mix. Take away any fresh food I have left from the day before. Put in some new fruit and vegetables. Check the water bottle.

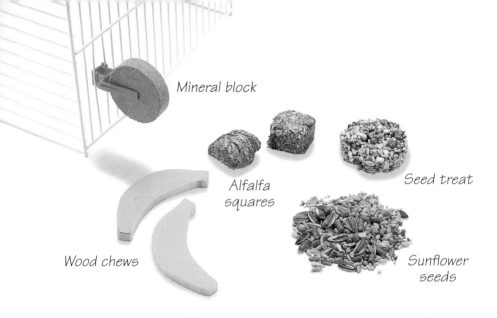

Mineral block

Alfalfa squares

Seed treat

Wood chews

Sunflower seeds

I can have one of these treats every day – not too much or I'll get fat! The banana-flavoured wood chews are for me to gnaw. The mineral block must stay in my cage.

Treats and Titbits

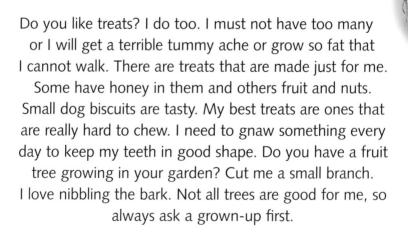

Do you like treats? I do too. I must not have too many or I will get a terrible tummy ache or grow so fat that I cannot walk. There are treats that are made just for me. Some have honey in them and others fruit and nuts. Small dog biscuits are tasty. My best treats are ones that are really hard to chew. I need to gnaw something every day to keep my teeth in good shape. Do you have a fruit tree growing in your garden? Cut me a small branch. I love nibbling the bark. Not all trees are good for me, so always ask a grown-up first.

I am going to hide some of this to eat later.

You can buy wood chews for me if you haven't got a tree. If I don't have things to gnaw, my teeth will get so long I will not be able to eat at all. You can hang a spray of millet in my cage. People buy them for their pet birds, but I like them too. Pet shops sell a mineral block for me. Please hang it in my cage and then I can nibble it whenever I need to. Remember to add pet vitamin drops to my food twice a week.

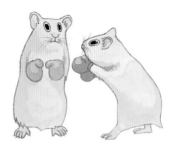

Living On My Own

I must explain something odd about me. You see, I don't like living with a friend – I only like living by myself. I know just how I want my home to be. I like my nest right here and my food bowl over there. I love storing my food in my nest. Then if I wake up and feel hungry, I can have a quick snack. I will not have to move far. I don't want to find anyone else eating MY food. I know where my water bottle is and nobody else must use it.

My eyes are bright and shiny, but I can only see things that are close to my nose, so I get a bit of a shock when something appears in front of me. That is when I might bite. I don't mean to. I can be grumpy – not with you – you are my friend. I just hate other hamsters. They annoy me. It is cruel to put two of us together. We just have to fight. We will hurt each other and one of us might die. Never leave me alone with your pet cat or dog. They just see me as a tasty snack.

Please try to make my home interesting. I enjoy climbing over logs, exploring cardboard tunnels, or simply scrabbling about in wood shavings.

Toys and Playtime

I might not want to play when I first come to live with you, but as soon as I learn that you will not hurt me, we will have really good fun together. You can buy toys for me from the pet shop. A wheel in my cage will make me think I am running a long way. May I have a solid wheel please? I might trap my toes in one that has gaps in it. When I am awake I rush around my cage looking for things to do. If you make me a mini-playground, I will have hours of fun playing in it.

I must not left in a plastic ball for too long as it makes me very tired.

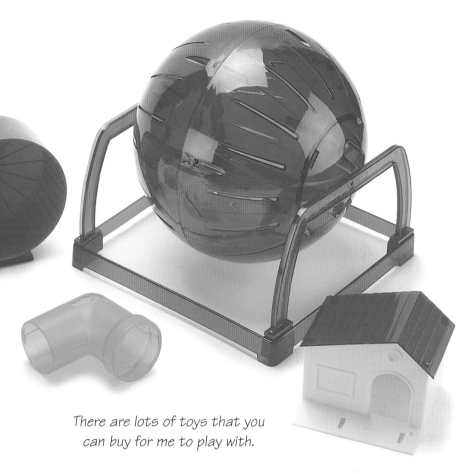

There are lots of toys that you can buy for me to play with.

I like to hide in things and love running through tunnels. A roll of cardboard will do. Push one end of the tube into the shavings. I can pretend I am in a burrow under the ground. Big plastic balls that you put me in are fun for you but they are not always fun for me. After 15 minutes I will be very tired. I like playing in the early morning or in the evening. We will just have time for a game before you go to school. We can play again when you get home.

Looking My Best

I spend a lot of time keeping my fur clean and shiny. You can help by brushing my hair. Only use a soft brush. I am very fussy about how I look. I can reach nearly every part of my body with my teeth, so I do not need brushing every day. I never, ever, need a bath. If I do get a little grubby, just wipe my fur with a bit of damp cottonwool.

One way to tell if I am upset about something is to watch me. I will clean and clean my fur if I am annoyed.

Don't brush too hard...ouch!

You do not have to buy me a big brush. A little one is fine. You can even use a soft, dry toothbrush. Please brush me gently – it hurts if you do it too hard. Start at my head and brush my fur the same way as it grows. Really hairy hamsters are much harder to look after. They will need brushing every day. You will have to buy a comb for them too. Hamsters don't need toothbrushes – I keep my teeth clean by chewing things. Raw carrot is a great tooth-cleaner. Apple or hazel wood is also good to chew and it looks after my teeth.

Only brush me in the direction in which my fur grows – from my head towards my tail.

Playing Indoors

I need to have lots of exercise. I get bored shut up in my cage with nothing to do. When I am really tame, you may think about letting me play outside my cage. First check the room in which I am going to run free. Is it safe for me? I am so tiny and I can run so fast that if I hide, you will not be able to see where I am. I can squeeze into tiny cracks. I might even get stuck. I sometimes chew my way into sofas or even into your bed.

Always wash your hands after playing with me.

I think that I am a super climber. I can climb high up the curtains. Whoops! I am not very good at getting down again. Can you rescue me? Your bedroom is the best place for play. Put a notice on the outside of the door that says "Hamster Loose". Then nobody will open the door and let me out. If I escape, you will have to make a trap to catch me. Put some bedding and food in the bottom of a bucket. Make a staircase from books next to it. If I climb up and get into the bucket, I will not be able to climb out again and you can rescue me.

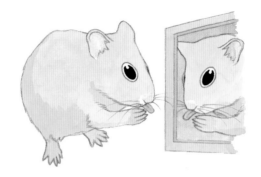

Visits To My Doctor

My doctor is called a veterinarian. Vet for short. They look after me if I am sick. When I am ill, you must get me to the vet fast. Do I keep scratching?
The vet will be able to tell you why I am so itchy. I may have fleas, lice or mites. The vet will give you something to put on my fur to make the horrid things go away.

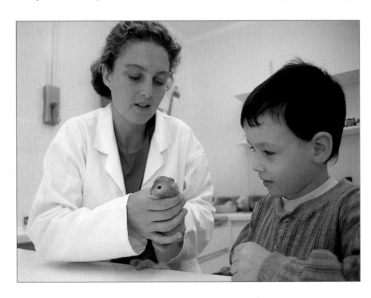

Feel my body for lumps or bumps – if you find one, take me to the vet.

There are other times when you should take me to the vet. I must go if I have a runny nose or eyes. Do I make a wheezy noise when I breathe? That will mean another visit to the vet. Every week you must feel my body for lumps and bumps. Rush me to the vet if my droppings are runny or if the fur under my tail is always wet. If my teeth or claws grow too long, the vet can cut them for me. I don't like it much, but I always feel a lot better when it has been done. I am very lucky, I do not have to have injections every year, like dogs and cats, to keep me safe from germs.

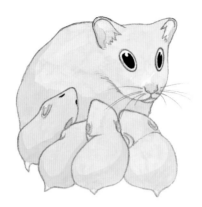

If I Have Babies

I do not want to have babies. Looking after them is very hard work for me. I will be much happier if I don't have any but, just in case I do, I will tell you how to look after us. I need a quiet place to look after them. I will need lots of extra bedding so I can build a bigger nest. I will probably have between five and seven babies, sometimes more.

My babies are born without any fur and their eyes are shut. I will feed them with my milk for about three weeks. Extra food then for me please so that I can make lots of milk. When the babies are tiny, do not try and touch them or me. I will think they are in danger and I might even kill them myself. Let the babies live with me until they are 25 days old. I will show them how to eat solid food. Then you must put each one into its own cage. The vet can tell you which ones are boys and which are girls. You can teach them how to be picked up and stroked. Then you can let them go to live with some new friends.

My Special Page

My name is
_____

My birthday is
_____

Am I a boy or a girl?
_____

_____

My colour is
_____

_____

Please put a
photograph or a
picture of me
here

The colour of my eyes is
_____

What breed am I?
_____

My favourite food is
_____

My favourite toy is
_____

My vet's phone number is
_____

Hamster Check List

1 Feed and water me every day.

2 Wash my bowls every day.

3 Check my eyes and ears are clean every day.

4 Check if I empty the food out of my pouches every day.

5 See that my fur and skin is clean every day.

6 Check my teeth every week.

7 Clean my cage really well every week.

8 Check my body for lumps and bumps every week.

9 See my claws are short with no splits.

10 Am I eating properly?

Syrian Hamsters

I have short hair. The colour of my fur is a lovely golden brown. I have a white tummy and little white patches of fur on my face. I think I am pretty. Do you? Friends that have a coat of all one colour are called self-coloured. Some have pale cream fur. If I had pure white hair and had pink eyes, I would be called an Albino. Some of us have coloured fur with patches of white in it. We are called piebald. Tortoiseshell hamsters have fur which is brown, yellow and red and they are always girls.

My friends that have soft, fluffy hair are called long-haired or "Teddy" hamsters. This sort of fur has to be brushed every day to keep it tidy and clean. Brushing the fur stops it from getting all messed up and tangled.

Other friends have very shiny fur and they are called "Satin" hamsters. If you get really keen on keeping us, you might like to take us to a show. Judges at the show will decide who is the best hamster and give him or her a prize. You will see lots of hamsters of all sorts of shapes, sizes and colours there.

A white stripe of fur around my middle is called a band.

Russian Dwarf Hamsters

I am a very small, round hamster. I am only about 10cm (4in) long even when I am fully grown. I think I am a cute little thing. Do you? My fur is a little bit longer than a Syrian's. I look like a ball of fluff. My hair is mostly grey. The fur on my tummy is white or a lighter grey. I often have a dark stripe of fur. It goes from the tip of my nose, along my back, to my little tail. I have white fur around my mouth and cheeks.

I am a bit easier to tame than my bigger
relatives. If you buy two baby brothers, we
can live together in a really big cage. We need
our own part of the cage to live in, mind you. I will
have my nest at one end of our house and my brother
can live at the other end. Sometimes you can have two
sisters living together, but they fight more than us boys
and can badly hurt each other. If I have babies – and
I really don't want them – there will be four or five of
them. I sometimes live a bit longer than other hamsters.

As I am so tiny,
cup me in your hands
to pick me up.

Chinese Hamsters

I am another small hamster. I grow to be about 12.5cm (5in) long. I have a longer tail than other hamsters. I can curl my tail round your finger to stop me falling off your hand. I look a little bit like a mouse – but I am not one!

My fur is quite short and smooth. It is a grey–brown colour. I have white hair on my tummy. There is a strip of black fur that starts on the top of my head. It runs along my back and ends at the top of my tail. I have small ears. They may have a tiny bit of black hair on the tips.

I use my whiskers to feel
for things in the dark.

I have a thinner body than my Syrian and Russian friends. I can squeeze through the tiniest gaps. Keep me in a cage that has glass or plastic sides or an old fish tank with a wire top. I can easily wriggle out through the gaps in wire cages. You can keep two brothers in the same large cage, but it is easier to keep only one hamster in one cage. I eat the same food as other hamsters, but I like to eat more green food and vegetables than some of my relatives.

A Note To Parents

Having pets is fun and the relationship between child and pet can be a magical one. I hope this book will encourage the new, young pet owner to look after their pet responsibly and enjoyably. Obviously parents will have to play a supervisory role, not only in daily care, but to explain that the new pet is a living being and not a toy. A well-cared-for pet is a happy one and will reward the whole family with unconditional love. Parents also have to bear the financial costs. Veterinary care can be eased with the help of Pet Health Insurance, well worth the annual premiums. Most veterinary clinics will have leaflets available.

Some of the subjects covered in this book may seem over-simplified to an adult, but I have tried to avoid too much technical detail. The subject of giving birth has been touched upon, but because of their aggressive attitude towards one another, hamsters are not the ideal pet for young children to breed. Hamsters are a wonderful little pets and are ideal for teaching children how to handle their pet friends gently. But please be aware that they are very short-lived. Two years is a good age for them. Three years is usually the maximum lifespan.

Acknowledgements

The author and publisher would like to thank the owners who generously allowed their pets to be photographed for this book, and the children who agreed to be models. Specifically they would like to thank Harriet de Freitas, Florence Elphick, Kate Elsom – and Peanut, Chloe Anderson – and Cookie, Sacha Wadey – and Toffee, Caroline Gosden, Sophie King and Claire Watson of Brinsbury College, Adversane – and Damascus, Ivan and Hong. Thanks also to Denis Blades of Gattleys, Storrington, Steyning Pet Shop, Pet Stop, Billingshurst, Neil Martin and Annika Sumner of Washington Garden Centre, Washington, Rolf C. Hagen (U.K.) Ltd., Christy Emblem at Interpet Ltd., and Farthings Veterinary Group, Billingshurst.

Thanks are due to the following photographers and picture libraries who kindly supplied photographs that are reproduced in this book.
Marc Henrie: 36, 44.
RSPCA Photolibrary: 9 bottom right (Angela Hampton), 18 (Angela Hampton), 28 (Angela Hampton), 34 (Tim Sambrook), 37 (Angela Hampton), 39 (Angela Hampton), 46 (Mike Lane).